Copyright © 2021 Chris Gibbs

First Edition

ISBN 978-1-9996363-6-4

Published by Inner Version Ltd
www.innerversion.com

# CXX — FIRST EXPERIENCE

I.  The personal beginning,
    The ignition of experience —
        To reach beneath the roots
            Is to access joy unbounded.


II. The contact with the infinite,
    The mountain incomplete —
        To venture into worlds unknown
            Is to feel with intuition.

# CXXI — UNBOUNDED THRESHOLD

I.  Before the categories,
    Beyond the names —
        Endures the ancient presence.

II. Between the words,
    Behind the signs —
        Unfurls the open space.

# CXXII — PRIMAL CALLING

I. The serene and higher calling
    Bellows with a whisper,
    Blazes with a sparkle.

II. The deep and primal path
    Unrolls with a meander,
    Guides with a caress.

# CXXIII — SILENT REVERSAL

I.  The rhythm of the past
    Invites the harmony of introspection.

II. The whispers of the world
    Surpass the loudest prophecies of promise.

# CXXIV — TIMELESS PORTAL

I. Central stillness in adventure
   Flows across the bridge.


II. Inner magic in connection
    Reaches through the gate.

# CXXV — ENTIRE COMFORT

I. No time is absent,
No task undone
    Within the fullness of the great unchanged.

II. The apprentice graciously
    Receives the boundless space,
    Rescinds the need to advertise
        Within expression of the all.

# CXXVI – NOTHING UNEXPLAINED

I. Every-thought contemplation
Considers all potential thought
   In an instant:
Thoughts remaining
   Fall away.


II. The release in meditation:
   Nothing unexplained,
   Liberated presence.

# CXXVII — UPLIFTED TRAVEL

I. Boundless rise
    Recovers with each leap
        Over doors of stale obsession.


II. Weightless travel
    Rediscovers pleasure
        With every twist and turn
    Through the clouds unburdened.

# CXXVIII – UNCHANGING PRESENCE

I.  The sensual ride
       Through light and dark
    Surrounds the centre of the stillness.

II. The balancing force
       In lull and thrust
    Sustains the life in full awareness.

# CXXIX — ETERNAL MOTION

I. The breathless voice
    Speaks quietly in pause
        Within the storm.


II. The burdened world
    Finds lightness in the realm
        Inside of time.

# CXXX — CLOSE EQUIVALENCE

I. Experience of the sacred
   Thunders into focus,
   Resonates the silence.

II. Renewal for the distance
   Bows in harmony,
   Extends the infinite.

# CXXXI — INNER WONDER

I. When infinity seems to cease,
   Inner search for light
       Extends toward the centre.

II. On finding joy is hampered,
    Golden beams of wonder
        Spear the darkest clouds.

# CXXXII — MAGICAL AWAKENING

I.     The central hearth in slumber
        Glows behind the veils —
    Endures with embers warm
        To the search beyond the temple.


II.     The silent store of magic
        Makes no sound directly —
    Echoes to patterns deep,
        Unique in resonance.

# CXXXIII — TREASURE WITHIN

I.  In creation uniquely forged
    Unveils the sacred essence.


II. In rise through darkness
    Unclouds the inner light.

# CXXXIV — CONTRASTING BRIGHTNESS

I. The instant world unfolding
    Gleams the timeless in the present
    Dance of real and magic.


II. The patient realm of meaning
    Glows the boundless in expanded
    Play of light and shadow.

# CXXXV — IDEAL INTERFACE

I.  The spotless mirror
    Gathers the distant rays,
    Hones with flawless focus
    In accordance with the source.


II. The clear water
    Feels the deeper knowledge,
    Reveals in proportion
    To the stillness of the surface.

# CXXXVI — DEEP FORGIVENESS

I. Discovery descends in yielding
    To the slowness of the ancient.


II. The deeper stillness
    Feels the surface stirring,
    Forgives the shallow effort
        Made in fast desire.

# CXXXVII — IMPERFECT WISDOM

I. Closed boxes of imperfection
    Lit by effort from within —
    Are blind to the effortless light
        Beyond the boundary.

II. The full illumination
    Sees the parts impure,
    Prevails with light opposing
        Through the centre.

# CXXXVIII — BOUNDLESS REVELATION

I.    Finite thoughts give way
        Upon discovering the key
            Embedded deep within.

II.    The image beyond effort
        Cradles the view of beauty
            Veiled by mundanity.

# CXXXIX — ETERNAL MAGIC

I.  The secret will of synchronicity
    Connects beyond the flow of time,
    Reaches in serene existence.

II. The hidden eye of mental alchemy
    Turns base ideas to golden flowers,
    Oversees the life transforming.

III. The briefest glimpse into the looking glass
    Reveals below the waking world,
    Emanates the deep adventure.

# CXL — ORIGINAL RESEARCH

I. No substitute
    For personal discovery
    Can equal the excitement
        In exploring subtle difference.

II. The searching beam
    Through the dark unique
    Sustains its purpose
        In revealing central place.

# CXLI — CLOSE BELONGING

I. Illumination in the central
    Holds no greater aspiration.

II. Detachment to the distance
    Amplifies the core possession.

# CXLII — AUTHENTIC MOUNTAIN

I.  To integrate the poles opposing
    Is to bring a ceaseless torch
    Into the caverns unexplored in person.

II.  To fulfil the inner myth
    Is to shine a guiding beacon
    From the summit unsurpassed in clarity.

# CXLIII — APPROACHING DAWN

I. The purest rays of morning sun
   Descend upon the silent spires.

II. The light reflected by example
    Filters through the waking valley.

# CXLIV — AWAKENED FRACTAL

I. Highest intention
    Contemplates the task unique,
    Reflects the partial view
        Towards the greater pattern.


II. Rising vibration
    Resonates on every level,
    Yields the upward path
        To endless resting motion.

# CXLV — MUTUAL ELEVATION

I.    The rise beyond the balcony above
        Inhales the sky ascending,
        Overflows in shared excess.

II.    The lift beneath the balcony below
        Improves from higher observation,
        Extends the common ground.

# CXLVI — PROMOTED JOY

I. Individual joy
   Respects the choice of difference.


II. Extended pleasure
   Promotes the path communal.

# CXLVII — SHARED CONNECTION

I. In exploring of uniqueness
    Comprehends the deep devotion.


II. In repeating of diplomacy
    Improves the firm foundation.

# CXLVIII — CALM EXCITEMENT

I. Calmness extends
  Below the deepest
    Depths of concentration.


II. Excitement lifts
  Above the loftiest
    Peaks of imagination.

# CXLIX — ARISING EVERYWHERE

I. The patience in awareness dwells
    Beneath the full potential.


II. The ecstasy of living soars
    Beyond the shared uniqueness.

# CL — NO CONFINEMENT

I.     To release the limits
        Is to pause temptation
        For the finite world
            In favour of the ancient recollection.

II.     To encourage full expression
        Is to gently
        Shift the wider view
            Towards the vital balance.

# CLI — OUTWARD OPENING

I. Transforming light of consciousness
   Unveils the inner radiance.

II. Outpouring of the life unbounded
    Opens to the vibrant world.

# CLII — INCREASING TRUST

I. Ascending paths
   Trust in their deepest source.

II. Connected intuition
   Rises through the stagnant doubt.

# CLIII — EFFORTLESS DISCOVERY

I. Creative rhythm
   Emanates from silence.

II. Eternal truth
   Requires no force.

# CLIV — SLOW VALUE

I. Real meaning
   Takes time to acquire.


II. Patient judgement
   Waits for wisdom overflowing.

# CLV — INFINITE COMPASSION

I. Eternal grace
    Ascends below the surface.


II. Unbounded presence
    Heals the great imbalance.

# CLVI — ENDURING SPIRIT

I.    Forgotten blooms of vapour
        Merge dependence in the downpour
            Over the ocean.


II.    Majestic towers of stone
        Relinquish difference in the sandstorm
            Across the desert.


III.    The fallen lives in waiting
        Strengthen patience in the airflow
            Through the forest.

# CLVII — ENDLESS YIELD

I. In the place where trails expire,
   Attention gathers on the centre.

II. When time can fall no further,
    Yields the infinite ascending.

# CLVIII — THE FOUNTAIN

I. The towering thrust of the stream
    Selected — heightens the potential
    For unique serenity
        Upon ascension in the sky.


II.       The sparkling descent of a thousand
    Droplets — guides the light in each
    Direction, merges with the boundless pool
Upon falling to the source.

# CLIX — ULTIMATE BEGINNING

I. Infinite expression
    Endlessly renews the potential
        For unbounded pleasure.


II. The time released
    In joy aspires
        To be an introduction.

| | |
|---|---|
| CXX — | FIRST EXPERIENCE |
| CXXI — | UNBOUNDED THRESHOLD |
| CXXII — | PRIMAL CALLING |
| CXXIII — | SILENT REVERSAL |
| CXXIV — | TIMELESS PORTAL |
| CXXV — | ENTIRE COMFORT |
| CXXVI — | NOTHING UNEXPLAINED |
| CXXVII — | UPLIFTED TRAVEL |
| CXXVIII — | UNCHANGING PRESENCE |
| CXXIX — | ETERNAL MOTION |
| CXXX — | CLOSE EQUIVALENCE |
| CXXXI — | INNER WONDER |
| CXXXII — | MAGICAL AWAKENING |
| CXXXIII — | TREASURE WITHIN |
| CXXXIV — | CONTRASTING BRIGHTNESS |
| CXXXV — | IDEAL INTERFACE |
| CXXXVI — | DEEP FORGIVENESS |
| CXXXVII — | IMPERFECT WISDOM |
| CXXXVIII — | BOUNDLESS REVELATION |
| CXXXIX — | ETERNAL MAGIC |

| | |
|---|---|
| CXL — | ORIGINAL RESEARCH |
| CXLI — | CLOSE BELONGING |
| CXLII — | AUTHENTIC MOUNTAIN |
| CXLIII — | APPROACHING DAWN |
| CXLIV — | AWAKENED FRACTAL |
| CXLV — | MUTUAL ELEVATION |
| CXLVI — | PROMOTED JOY |
| CXLVII — | SHARED CONNECTION |
| CXLVIII — | CALM EXCITEMENT |
| CXLIX — | ARISING EVERYWHERE |
| CL — | NO CONFINEMENT |
| CLI — | OUTWARD OPENING |
| CLII — | INCREASING TRUST |
| CLIII — | EFFORTLESS DISCOVERY |
| CLIV — | SLOW VALUE |
| CLV — | INFINITE COMPASSION |
| CLVI — | ENDURING SPIRIT |
| CLVII — | ENDLESS YIELD |
| CLVIII — | THE FOUNTAIN |
| CLIX — | ULTIMATE BEGINNING |

www.ingramcontent.com/pod-product-compliance
Lightning Source LLC
Chambersburg PA
CBHW071409070526
44578CB00002B/532